INDIAN ARCHITECTURE AND ORNAMENT

INDIAN ARCHITECTURE AND ORNAMENT

LOCKWOOD DE FOREST

GYAN

Published by

Gyan Publishing House
5, Ansari Road
Daryaganj, New Delhi-110002
Phone: 011-47034999, 9811692060
E-mail: books@gyanbooks.com

Distribution Network
gyanbooks.com
India, USA, Canada, UK, Australia

ISBN: 978-93-6920-519-6 (HB)

First Published, 1887

2nd Impression 2025

Printed at: Gyan Press, Delhi.

INDIAN ARCHITECTURE AND ORNAMENT
Author: LOCKWOOD DE FOREST

INDIAN ARCHITECTURE AND ORNAMENT

INTRODUCTION.

I have given the following examples of Indian Architecture as nearly every traveller would see them, beginning with Ahmedabad nearest to Bombay, and ending with Multan. As will be seen, this does not follow the chronological order, but rather the gradual change from the Hindoo to the Mohammedan style, as one goes North, and only includes the period from A. D. 1236 to the present time. In Ahmedabad the mosques are built of yellow sandstone, and they are all purely Jain in detail, often constructed entirely from older Jain temples. This gives them a peculiar style of their own, and they form one of the most interesting groups in the whole of India. Here, too, the stone tracery has been brought to its highest perfection. The old palace is a strange contrast, showing no trace of Jain influence. The date of these buildings is 1391 to 1583. I would call special attention to the construction of the houses; it is the best I have ever seen, being a heavy-timbered frame, with a second one inside, some three feet from the outside one, and the two bound together with beams which show both inside and out. The whole is filled in with stucco. Teak, the wood used, is certainly the most durable in the world. The very elaborate carving of the fronts and court yards lasts for centuries. I have examples which have been exposed to the weather for over two hundred years, and they are as sound as the day they were put up. The climate is much more severe on wood than our own, which we think the worst to be found. The lasting qualities of Teak are due to the wood being full of natural oil which never dries out, so that any filler, oil, varnish or paint is entirely unnecessary. Shet Huttusing temple, built some forty years ago, Furgusson speaks of as the finest modern building and the clearest proof that native architecture is not dead. I am a little doubtful about the houses attributed to Ajmir, as they may be at Lahore or Amritza. They show the curious mixture of the Hindoo and Mohammedan in the same work. The palace at Amber, the old capital of Jeypore, contains the finest examples of Shish work in India. No one who has not seen this wonderful inlay of mirror pieces can form any conception of its beauty. They are cut from large glass globes, which gives each piece a convex surface, entirely removing all idea of looking-glass. The effect is more that of rounded surfaces of polished steel. I would refer the reader to Fursson's Indian Architecture for descriptions of Akbar's Palace at Futtehpur Sikri, the Palace at Agra, and the tombs and Palace at Delhi. The examples of houses at Amritza Lahore and Multan are as interesting in their style as those of Ahmedabad, though inferior in their construction. The Shisham and Deodar are substituted for the Teak, which does not grow much north of Bombay. The very odd little bay windows are rather the feature of the Lahore streets, while one is struck by the great beauty of the red sandstone doorways in Multan. In the study of Architecture in the East the houses have been neglected, so we find few illustrations of them. I think they are really more instructive than many of the mosques and temples. No country affords a greater variety than India, where each city has its own peculiarities in detail and plan. I can only hope that I have been able to stimulate in some, at least, the desire to know more of this wonderful Oriental art which is so rapidly disappearing.

LOCKWOOD DE FOREST.

CONTENTS.

I.

GEO. H. POLLEY & CO., PUBLISHERS, BOSTON.

MOSQUE AT AHMEDABAD.

GEO. H. POLLEY & CO., PUBLISHERS, BOSTON.

MOOHAFIZ KAHN'S MOSQUE, AHMEDABAD.

GEO. H. POLLEY & CO., PUBLISHERS, BOSTON

DETAILS RANI SIPRE MOSQUE. AHMEDABAD.

IV.

GEO. H. POLLEY & CO., PUBLISHERS, BOSTON.

NICHE, RANI SIPRE MOSQUE, AHMEDABAD.

GEO. H. POLLEY & CO., PUBLISHERS, BOSTON.

CIRCULAR BAY WINDOW OF A HOUSE. AHMEDABAD.

GEO. H. POLLEY & CO., PUBLISHERS, BOSTON.

BAY WINDOW OF A HOUSE, AHMEDABAD.

GEO. H. POLLEY & CO., PUBLISHERS, BOSTON.

HOUSE AT AHMEDABAD.

GEO. H POLLEY & CO., PUBLISHERS, BOSTON.

DOOR OF THE OLD PALACE, (USED AS THE JAIL,) AHMEDABAD.

GEO. H. POLLEY & CO., PUBLISHERS, BOSTON.

INTERIOR OF THE OLD PALACE, AHMEDABAD.

GEO. H. POLLEY & CO., PUBLISHERS, BOSTON.

SHET HUTTUSING TEMPLE, AHMEDABAD.

GEO. H. POLLEY & CO., PUBLISHERS, BOSTON.

DETAILS OF THE FRONT OF A HOUSE, AJMIR.

GEO. H. POLLEY & CO., PUBLISHERS, BOSTON.

BAY WINDOW OF A HOUSE. AJMIR.

GEO. H. POLLEY & CO., PUBLISHERS, BOSTON.

BAY WINDOW OF A HOUSE, AJMIR.

GEO. H POLLEY & CO., PUBLISHERS, BOSTON.

DOOR OF THE PALACE AT AMBER.

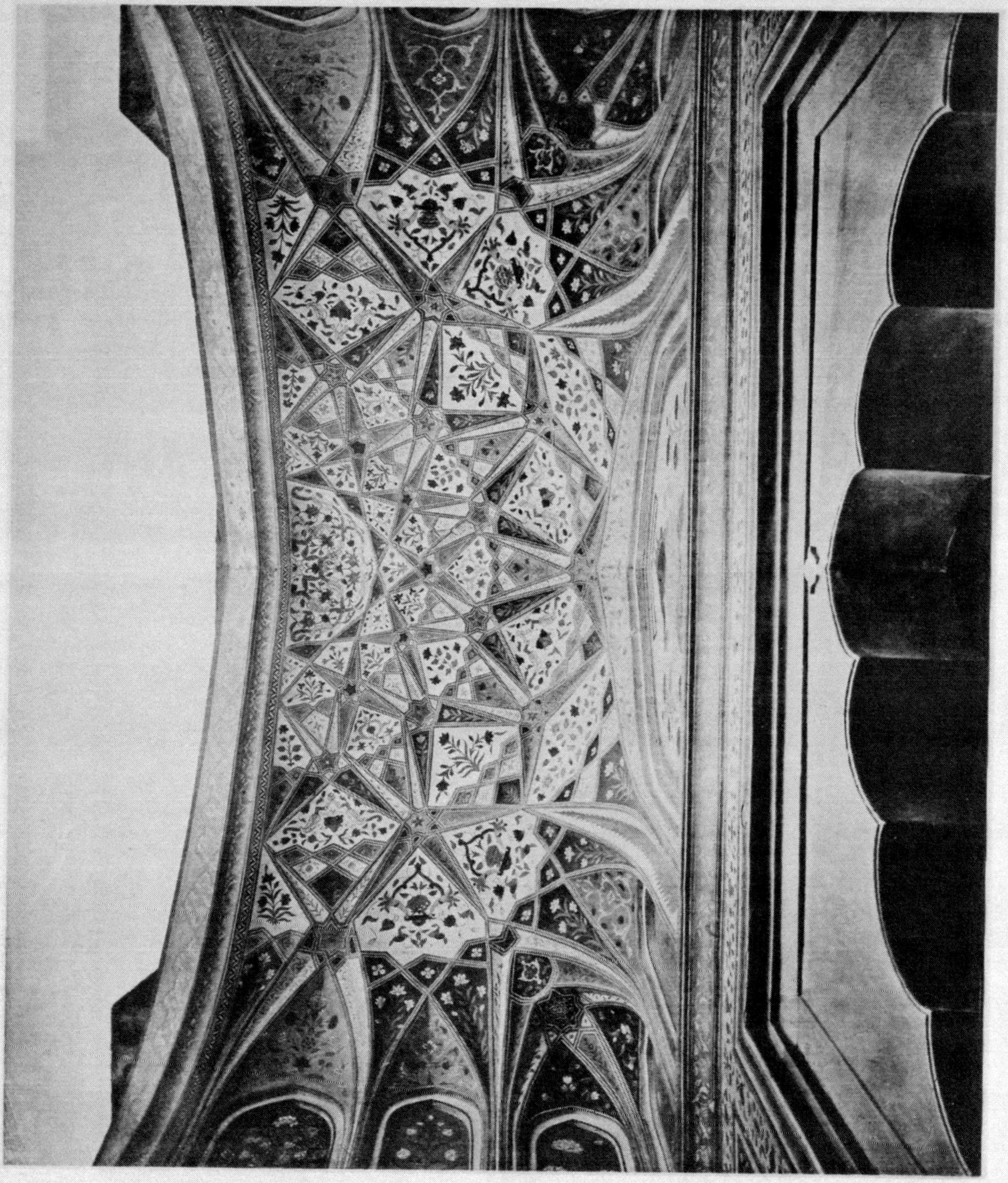

GEO. H. POLLEY & CO., PUBLISHERS, BOSTON.

CEILING, DOORWAY OF PALACE, AMBER.

GEO. H. POLLEY & CO., PUBLISHERS, BOSTON

COURT OF THE PALACE, AMBER.

THE WALLS ARE COVERED WITH SHISH WORK.

XVII.

GEO. H. POLLEY & CO., PUBLISHERS, BOSTON.

CEILING OF SHISH WORK, AMBER.

XVIII

GEO. H. POLLEY & CO., PUBLISHERS, BOSTON.

ROOM IN THE PALACE, AMBER, WALLS AND CEILING OF SHISH WORK.

GEO. H. POLLEY & CO., PUBLISHERS, BOSTON.

OLD DOOR IN THE PALACE, AMBER.

GEO. H. POLLEY & CO., PUBLISHERS, BOSTON.

OLD DOOR IN THE PALACE, AMBER.

XXI.

GEO. H. POLLEY & CO., PUBLISHERS, BOSTON.

THE SULTANA'S KIOSK, AKBAR'S PALACE, FUTTEHPORE SIKRI.

XXII.

GEO. H. POLLEY & CO., PUBLISHERS, BOSTON

ZENANA IN THE PALACE AT AGRA, SHAH JEHAN.

WHITE MARBLE INLAID WITH PRECIOUS STONES.

GEO. H. POLLEY & CO., PUBLISHERS, BOSTON.

ZENANA PAVILION, PALACE AT AGRA.

XXIV.

GEO. H. POLLEY & CO., PUBLISHERS, BOSTON

TOMB OF ALTUMSH, OLD DELHI.

XXV.

GEO. H. POLLEY & CO., PUBLISHERS, BOSTON.

INTERIOR OF THE TOMB OF ALA UD-DIN KHILJI.

XXVI.

GEO. H POLLEY & CO., PUBLISHERS, BOSTON.

INTERIOR OF A TOMB, OLD DELHI.

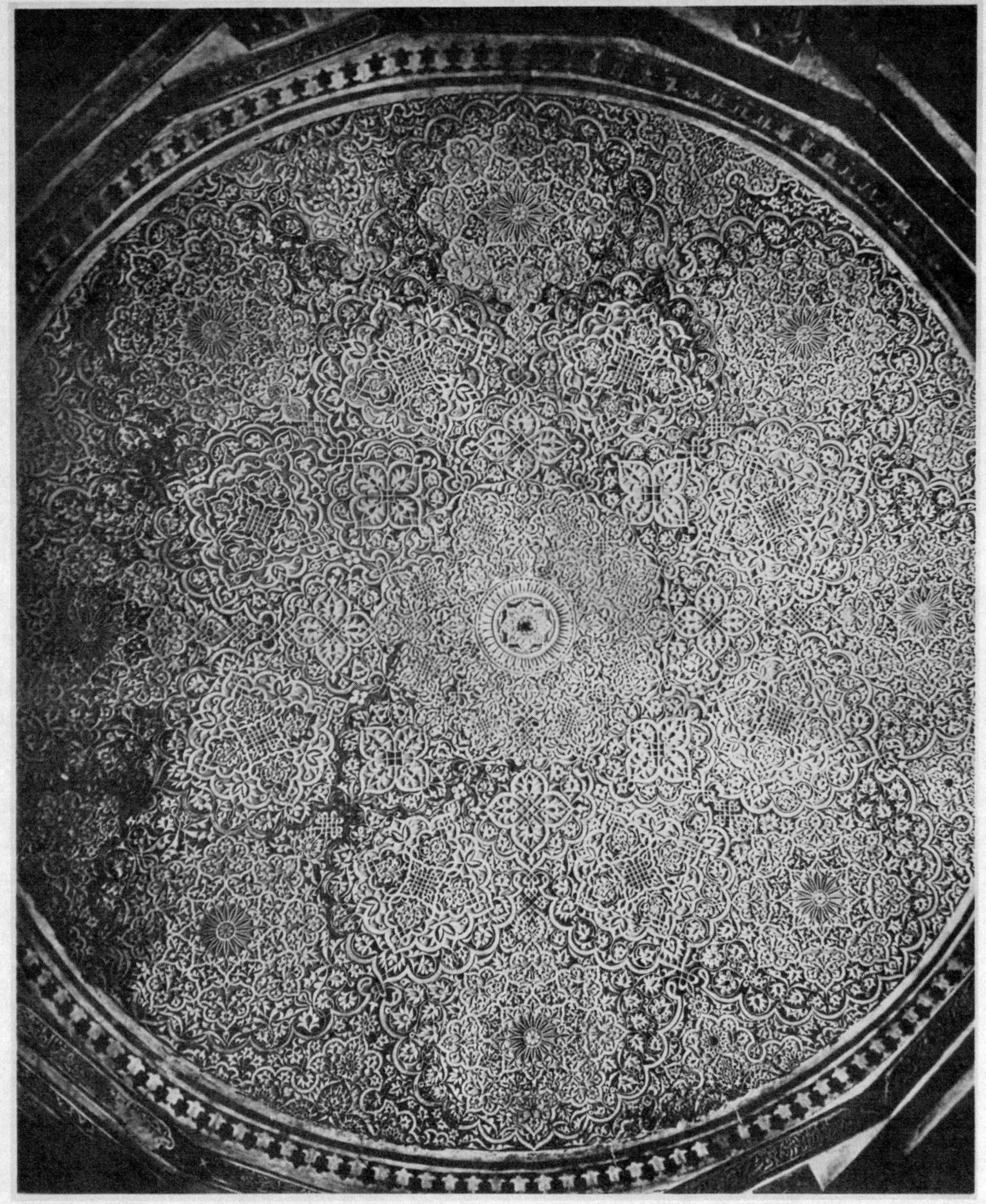

GEO. H. POLLEY & CO., PUBLISHERS, BOSTON.

CEILING OF A TOMB, OLD DELHI.

XXVIII.

GEO. H. POLLEY & CO., PUBLISHERS, BOSTON.

INTERIOR OF A MOSQUE. BRICK TILE AND MOSAIC WORK.

GEO. H. POLLEY & CO., PUBLISHERS, BOSTON.

INTERIOR OF THE SAME MOSQUE.

INTERIOR OF THE PALACE DELHI.

XXXI.

GEO. H. POLLEY & CO., PUBLISHERS, BOSTON.

HOUSE IN THE BAZAR, AMRITZA.

XXXII.

GEO. H. POLLEY & CO., PUBLISHERS, BOSTON.

WINDOW OF A HOUSE, AMRITZA.

XXXIII.

GEO. H. POLLEY & CO., PUBLISHERS, BOSTON.

BAY WINDOW AT AMRITZA.

XXXIV.

GEO. H POLLEY & CO., PUBLISHERS, BOSTON.

WINDOW AT AMRITZA.

GEO. H. POLLEY & CO., PUBLISHERS, BOSTON.

INLAID MARBLE SIKH WORK, AMRITZA.

GEO. H. POLLEY & CO., PUBLISHERS, BOSTON.

GILDED COPPER DOORS, SIKH WORK, AMRITZA.

GEO. H. POLLEY & CO., PUBLISHERS, BOSTON.

DOME OF THE GREAT MOSQUE, LAHORE. JEHAN GIR.

GEO. H. POLLEY & CO., PUBLISHERS, BOSTON.

CEILING IN THE GREAT MOSQUE, LAHORE.

GEO. H. POLLEY & CO., PUBLISHERS, BOSTON.

STREET IN THE BAZAR, LAHORE.

GEO. H. POLLEY & CO., PUBLISHERS, BOSTON.

BAY WINDOW, LAHORE.

GEO. H. POLLEY & CO., PUBLISHERS, BOSTON.

OLD BAY WINDOW IN THE MUSEUM, LAHORE.

XLII.

GEO. H. POLLEY & CO., PUBLISHERS, BOSTON

HOUSE AT LAHORE.

XLIII.

GEO. H POLLEY & CO., PUBLISHERS, BOSTON

INTERIOR OF A HOUSE, PROBABLY MULTAN.

GEO. H. POLLEY & CO., PUBLISHERS, BOSTON.

DOORWAY, PUNJAB.

GEO. H. POLLEY & CO., PUBLISHERS, BOSTON.

DOOR OF THE GREAT MOSQUE, MULTAN.

XLVI.

GEO. H. POLLEY & CO., PUBLISHERS, BOSTON.

TOMB AT MULTAN, GLAZED TILES.

XLVII.

GEO. H. POLLEY & CO., PUBLISHERS, BOSTON.

DETAILS OF TOMB AT MULTAN.

XLVIII.

GEO. H. POLLEY & CO., PUBLISHERS, BOSTON.

HOUSE AT MULTAN.

GEO. H. POLLEY & CO., PUBLISHERS, BOSTON.

DOORWAY OF A HOUSE AT MULTAN.

GEO. H. POLLEY & CO., PUBLISHERS, BOSTON.

DOORWAY OF A HOUSE AT MULTAN.